GETTING TO KNOW THE WORLD'S GREATEST ARTISTS

H E N R I
MATISSE

WRITTEN AND ILLUSTRATED BY MIKE VENEZIA

CHILDREN'S PRESS®
A DIVISION OF GROLIER PUBLISHING
NEW YORK   LONDON   HONG KONG   SYDNEY
DANBURY, CONNECTICUT

Cover: *Horse Rider and Clown*, from the portfolio *Jazz*, by Henri Matisse.
Paris, Editions Verve, 1947. Pochoir, printed in color, composition.
42.2 x 65.6 cm. ©1996 The Museum of Modern Art, New York,
Gift of the Artist. © ARS, NY.

Project Editor: Shari Joffe
Design: Steve Marton

Library of Congress Cataloging–in–Publication Data

Venezia, Mike.
        Henri Matisse / written and illustrated by Mike Venezia.
            p. cm. — (Getting to know the world's greatest artists)
        Summary: Discusses the life and work of French post-impressionist
artist Henri Matisse.
        ISBN 0-516-20311-8 (lib. bdg.)   0-516-26146-0 (pbk.)
        1. Matisse, Henri, 1869–1954 —Juvenile literature. 2. Artists–
France—Biography—Juvenile literature. [1. Matisse, Henri, 1869–1954.
2. Artists. 3. Art appreciation.] I. Title. II. Series: Venezia, Mike.
Getting to know the world's greatest artists.
N6853.M33V46   1997
709`.2—dc20
[B]
                                                        96-28557
                                                          CIP
                                                          AC

Self Portrait, by Henri Matisse. 1906. Statens Museum for Kunst, Copenhagen, Denmark. Photograph by Hans Petersen. © ARS, NY.

Henri Matisse was one of the most important painters of the twentieth century. He said he wanted his artwork to give people pleasure, and be soothing—kind of like a comfortable armchair you can rest in after a hard day's work.

The Goldfish, by Henri Matisse. 1911. Oil on canvas. 57 7/8 x 38 5/8 in. Pushkin Museum of Fine Arts, Moscow, Russia. Scala/Art Resource, NY. © ARS, NY.

Open Window, by Henri Matisse. 1905. Oil on canvas. The Collection of Mrs. John Hay Whitney. Photograph © Jim Strong Inc. © ARS, NY.

Henri Matisse's greatest works do just what he wanted. By perfectly balancing simple shapes and beautiful colors, his paintings seem to make you feel good all over.

Sometimes Henri added decorative lines and colorful patterns to his paintings. He often let the plain white canvas show through in spots to give his colors a bright, sparkling feel.

Still Life in Seville II, by Henri Matisse. 1911. Oil on canvas. 35 x 45.5 in. The Hermitage Museum, St. Petersburg, Russia. Scala/Art Resource, NY. © ARS, NY.

Woman in Kimono, by Henri Matisse. Private Collection. Art Resource, NY. © ARS, NY.

Henri Matisse was born in the north of France, at Le Cateau-Cambresis, in 1869. Unlike most great artists, Henri didn't show the least bit of interest in art while he was growing up.

His parents owned a general store that sold seeds, grain, and household goods. Henri's father expected him to either work at the store or become a lawyer when he grew up. Henri ended up going to law school, but found it really boring.

It wasn't until Henri was twenty years old that he discovered how much he loved art. While Henri was recovering from a very serious illness called appendicitis, his mother gave him a box of paints so he would have something to do.

This was the most important moment in Henri Matisse's life. Suddenly he was no longer bored. Henri found out he loved to paint!

After he got better, Henri got a job as
an assistant lawyer in his town. He took
some art courses early in the morning before
work started. Soon he was spending more
and more time drawing and painting.

Iris, by Henri Matisse. 1886–87. Pencil, ink and watercolor on paper. 17.1 x 22.1 cm. © Succession Henri Matisse, Musée Matisse, Nice, France. Photograph © Ville de Nice. © ARS, NY.

Henri even painted flowers on the legal documents he was supposed to file away! It didn't take long for Henri to decide to become a full-time artist. Henri's parents weren't very happy about his decision. His father was especially upset.

Nature Morte aux Livres, by Henri Matisse. 1890. Oil on canvas. 21.5 x 27 cm. © Succession Henri Matisse, Musée Matisse, Nice, France. Photograph © Ville de Nice. © ARS, NY.

Henri was so excited, though, that he finally talked his parents into letting him study art at a famous art school in Paris, France.

Because Henri Matisse hadn't become interested in art until he was an adult, he had a lot of catching up to do. He worked very hard studying all the things he would need to know to be a good artist. He learned about things like figure drawing, perspective, and composition.

During Henri Matisse's time, art schools taught students to paint in a style that everybody was used to seeing. These schools believed in certain rules that hadn't changed in years.

Art students were instructed to paint carefully drawn figures and objects in dark colors, like the painting on the next page. Although Henri enjoyed many of these works, he kept thinking there might be something new he could do to freshen up his own paintings.

Henri had a pretty rough time at art school. He failed some important exams, and didn't get along with most of his teachers. Fortunately, one of Henri's teachers took a special interest in him. Gustave Moreau was sure Henri Matisse could become a great artist someday. Gustave encouraged Henri to try new things and use his imagination as much as possible.

Saying Grace, by Jean-Baptiste Simeon Chardin. c. 1740. Oil on canvas.
19.5 x 15.25 in. Louvre, Paris, France. Giraudon/Art Resource, NY.

Henri Matisse often traveled to find new
and interesting things to paint. He usually
went to places that were bright and sunny.

Approaching of the Storm, by Camille Pissarro. Galleria d'Arte
Moderna, Florence, Italy. Scala/Art Resource, NY.

On one trip, he was introduced to an
Impressionist artist named John Russell.
Henri became very interested in the way
Russell used bright dabs of color.

Henri began to study other Impressionist painters, like Claude Monet and Camille Pissarro. Soon he began to add more colors in his own paintings. In *The Dinner Table*, Henri added beautiful flecks of color to the flowers, fruit, and glassware. This was the beginning of a whole new style of painting for Henri.

La Desserte, by Henri Matisse. 1897. Oil on canvas. 100 x 131 cm.
Private Collection. Bridgeman/Art Resource, NY. © ARS, NY.

La Cour du Moulin à Ajaccio, by Henri Matisse. 1898. Oil on canvas. 38.5 x 46 cm.
Sucession Henri Matisse, Musée Matisse, Nice, France. Photograph © Ville de Nice.
© ARS, NY.

Henri Matisse loved the new colors he put in his paintings. He decided to leave art school and try painting his own way. As he went along, his colors became brighter and brighter. For a while, he tried using hundreds of brushstrokes of bright colors.

Some of Henri's artist friends thought his new paintings were great. One of them, Paul Signac, liked the painting below so much that he bought it from Henri. But Henri wasn't satisfied with his new style. He wanted to experiment more with color, and try using larger shapes and thick lines of paint to make his works more expressive.

Luxe, Calme et Volupte, by Henri Matisse. 1904. Oil on canvas. 98.5 x 118.5 cm. Musee d'Orsay, Paris, France. Erich Lessing/Art Resource, NY. © ARS, NY.

The Family of the Artist, by Henri Matisse. 1911. Oil on canvas. 56 x 76 in. The Hermitage Museum, St. Petersburg, Russia. Scala/Art Resource, NY. © ARS, NY.

During the years Henri was experimenting with his art, he wasn't able to sell many paintings at all. Henri was married by this time. He and his wife, Amélie, had two sons. Henri also had a daughter from a previous relationship.

Amélie did everything she could to help her husband. Besides raising their family, she also modeled for Henri and worked in a hat shop to make extra money. The Matisses were so poor and hungry at this time that Henri said he was often tempted to eat the fruit he used as models for his still-life paintings.

Woman with the Hat,
by Henri Matisse. 1905.
Oil on canvas. 80.6 x 59.7 cm.
San Francisco Museum of
Modern Art, Bequest
of Elise S. Haas. © ARS, NY.

In 1905, Henri Matisse and some artist
friends entered their latest colorful paintings
in a show. These paintings started an uproar!

People were shocked. They thought these artists just slopped wild colors on the canvas. They were especially angry about Henri's painting of Amélie wearing a hat. Some people were so insulted that they wanted to destroy the paintings.

A writer who saw the show named the artists the *Fauves*, a French word that means "wild beasts." It didn't seem like a very nice name, but Henri and his friends didn't really mind it that much.

Portrait of Mme. Matisse, by Henri Matisse. 1905. Oil on canvas. 40.5 x 32.5 cm.
Statens Museum for Kunst, Copenhagen, Denmark. © ARS, NY.

The Fauve period lasted only a short time
for Henri Matisse. He was more interested
in looking for new ways to improve his art.

Henri started to move away from the bright, clashing colors he used in *Portrait of Mme. Matisse*. He began to use calmer colors and lots of decorative lines. In *The Joy of Life*, Henri was able to create a more soothing, dream-world kind of painting.

The Joy of Life, by Henri Matisse. 1905–06. Oil on canvas. 175 x 241 cm.
© The Barnes Foundation. © ARS, NY.

On one of his many trips, Henri visited Algeria, a sunny North African country. Henri saw lots of exciting designs on carpets, wallpaper, and people's clothing there. He began to add these decorative designs to his paintings.

In *Harmony in Red*, Henri used these designs to arrange the flat surface of his painting. It's interesting to compare this painting to the earlier one shown on page 17. It is about the same subject, but looks very different.

In 1908, a wealthy businessman named Sergei Shchukin bought *Harmony in Red*. Not many people understood Henri Matisse's paintings at this time, but Sergei loved almost everything Henri painted. In 1910, Sergei asked Henri to do a large painting for the hallway of his mansion.

Harmony in Red (The Tablecloth), by Henri Matisse. 1908. Oil on canvas. 70 7/8 x 86 5/8 in.
The Hermitage Museum, St. Petersberg, Russia. Scala/Art Resource, NY. © ARS, NY.

Henri Matisse created *Dance* for the large hallway. It is one of the most important paintings of modern times. Henri used very simple, flat shapes and bright colors. He chose

the bluest of blues for the sky and the greenest of greens for the earth. He used red for the dancers to show their energy.

Without using any of the carefully drawn figures, perspective, or natural colors used by artists of the past, Henri Matisse was able to show the excitement and joy of life. The dancers seem like they're about to burst out of the picture at any moment.

In his later years, when most artists start to slow down, Henri surprised people by creating art that was fresher and more colorful than ever before!

When he was older and had trouble standing at his easel, Henri switched to a new form of art that could be done sitting

Interior with Egyptian Curtain, by Henri Matisse. 1948. Oil on canvas. 116.2 x 89.2 cm. The Phillips Collection, Washington, D.C. © ARS, NY.

The Sadness of the King, by Henri Matisse. 1952. Oil on canvas. Musée National d'Arte Moderne, Paris, France. Erich Lessing / Art Resource, NY. © ARS, NY.

The Red Studio, by Henri Matisse. 1911. Oil on canvas, 181 x 219.1 cm. © 1997 The Museum of Modern Art, New York, Mrs. Simon Guggenheim Fund. © ARS, NY.

down. Henri cut out shapes from brightly colored paper to make some of his most exciting art ever. Henri said it was like drawing with scissors and sculpting with color.

Henri Matisse lived to be 84 years old. By the time he died, his artwork was known all over the world.

Henri Matisse in front of the stained glass window he designed for the Chapelle du Rosaire, Vence, France, 1950. Photograph by Dmitri Kessel, *Life Magazine.* © Time.

As an artist, Henri Matisse was much more than a painter. He was famous for his sculptures and line drawings, too. In 1948, he designed an entire chapel. Henri used all his talents to create the stained-glass windows, murals on the walls, floor designs, furniture, and even the priest's robes.

The works of art in this book come from:

Galleria d'Arte Moderna, Florence, Italy

The Hermitage Museum, St. Petersburg, Russia

The Louvre, Paris, France

Musee d'Orsay, Paris, France

Museum of Modern Art, New York

The Phillips Collection, Washington, D.C.

Pushkin Museum of Fine Arts, Moscow, Russia

San Francisco Museum of Modern Art

Statens Museum for Kunst, Copenhagen, Denmark

Succession Henri Matisse, Musee Matisse, Nice, France